His Beloved

JADE JUANA POLLY

THE WRITER WRITES

To know Him is to let Him know you.

To my family—thank you for standing with me through every valley, for holding me up when I wanted to fall. Thank you for the love that never wavered, the prayers I never heard but God did, and the constant reminder that I was never alone. Your faith in me has been an anchor, and your love has been a covering.

To those who listened when these words were still just drafts —thank you. Thank you for creating space for me to share what only God knew. For lending your ears, your hearts, and your honest thoughts. For encouraging me to keep going even when I questioned if these words mattered.

To those who witnessed these words firsthand—you know the weight they carry. You saw the battle before the breakthrough, the storm before the stillness. Thank you for seeing me, for reminding me that nothing is ever wasted in God's hands.

To the prodigals—there is room for you here. No matter how far you've wandered, how lost you feel, how much time you think has been wasted—His love is relentless. His arms are still open.

To those who want to speak up but feel shame—this is for you. I know what it's like to feel silenced by guilt, to believe the lie that your story is too messy, too broken, too unworthy to be told. But let me remind you—shame is not your portion. The enemy wants you to stay quiet, but God is calling you to freedom. There is power in your testimony, healing in your truth, and grace that covers it all. You are not too far gone. You are not disqualified. Speak, heal, and walk boldly in the love that has always been yours.

And to you, the reader—thank you for picking up this book, for opening these pages, for seeking something deeper. My prayer is that *His Beloved* reminds you that you are seen, known, and deeply loved. May His voice be louder than your doubts, and may you discover or rediscover the beauty of His love in ways you never expected.

This book is not just mine—it belongs to every heart willing to receive His truth.

Foreword

The blurry night intoxicated with all the brown liquor in the house and high on what was brought to me, I cried out for His help. As my body denied my will, I remembered my spirit could fight for me. It fought even though it came late in my eyes. It fought even though it did not prevent what happened next. His Spirit came in the midst and calmed the storm.

Looking back, I see how we throw ourselves into the deep end before calling on God. We walk in the opposite direction, into places He never sent us, into beds He never permitted us to be in. And then we sit in the consequences, feeling the full weight of our decisions. We let our trauma define who God is, let our pain narrate a story He never authored. We move through life without considering the One who created us, the One who has a purpose far beyond what we see. And still, when we hit rock bottom, when the darkness becomes unbearable, we know—some of us know—we can run to Him. *But maybe, some of us don't.*

I wrestled with believing God loved me because He knows everything. How could the God who sees all, see my suffering and not intervene? It felt like He didn't care. Like I was too far gone for Him to reach. The deeper the pain, the quieter I became. The deeper the pain, the more guilt and shame choked me. How can a good God love so deeply yet allow suffering?

As you walk through the pages of *His Beloved*, I ask one thing of you: let your walls come down. Soften your heart. Listen for His voice. He will speak. The question is—will you listen?

His Beloved:

"Lying back on Jesus' chest was one of His disciples, whom Jesus loved."
John 13:23 (NASB)

Abba

Yeshua

Helper

Abba

ABBA (Ăb′ bà) Aramaic word for "father" used by Jesus to speak of His own intimate relationship with God, a relationship that others can enter through faith. — *Holman Illustrated Bible Dictionary*

They call You Father,
but it feels foreign on my tongue,
a word I've heard so many times,
yet still, it escapes me.
It's like trying to wear someone else's skin,
too big, too small,
uncomfortable and unfamiliar.
I've never known a father
like the one they speak of.
My heart searches for the warmth
I've only heard about in stories.
The love they speak of,
the protection,
the unshakeable presence—
they say You offer all these,
but I've never felt them like they do.

So when I say "Father,"
it comes out hesitantly,
as if testing the waters
of a relationship I'm not sure I'm ready for.
Is it possible for someone like me
to truly call You that and mean it?
Or will I always feel like an outsider
trying to belong to a family
I wasn't sure was ever really mine?
I want to believe,
I want to trust in Your fatherhood,
but each time I speak Your name,
it still feels foreign on my tongue.
A part of me longs for it to fit,
longs for that intimacy,
longs for the truth behind the word.

To say I belong to You feels false,

> when I don't believe it anymore.

To say I am your child,

> when I act every way opposite to You
> seems contradictory

I am fighting to believe what they used to tell me,

> but it's not working.
> I gaslight myself hoping if I play along
> eventually I won't have to play.

I am trying to pull on what I have heard,
but I am only catching air.

It's not clicking.
> It's not making sense to me.
> I believed because I saw them believe
> and what that belief meant.

But if we are being honest,
> their belief isn't resonating with me.

> It hasn't settled on me.

> I am not an unbeliever, just a questioning one.
> I need to know You for me.
> I need to know You.

I want to know You.

But do You want to know me?

I am bewildered at that thought.
    I am frightened for You to know the depths of my being.

    I am terrified my questions will make You avoid me.
    I am terrified my questions will cause You to hate me.
    I am terrified my questions will make them exile me.

    I am afraid of You seeing I am more broken than whole

                    more tormented than happy.

    I am afraid of You seeing me smile knowing I had to practice
it before coming to speak with You.

    I am afraid of You seeing me.

So before You respond, can I preface?

I have experienced more life than I have lived.

I have experienced more Hollywood plots than I care to admit.

    I have experienced doubt in You, though I tattooed Your
    words on my wrist.

I don't know, though.

Saying I am Yours and believing it are two different things. One is effortless, and the other is convicting me.

I am more writer than talker.

So, I write to You

because tears are the only things

that come out when I want to speak.

My tongue is tied by past sins and hurt.
My mind is flooded by "what ifs" and "should haves,"
so if You wonder why I stopped,
it's because it's hard for me to
press

through

it.

Its an overwhelming feeling of pain that I haven't come to grips with yet. I am managing it though. *I think.* I am working through it so when we do talk, I know what to say to You.

I'm just not there yet.
I am trying to get there,
but I'm not
ready
yet.

I need to practice.

I've always
    wanted to
    share
    me
    with
    You.

I wanted
    to bring
    my flawed self
    into
    Your
    open arms
    but felt shame
    for being like this.

You know?
    Broken...

I messed up not once,
    not twice,
    but more times
    than I actually
    want to admit.
    I say,
    "I am the
    chosen one."

They chose me
    for one reason,
    and it was the wrong one.

. . .

I've been lying.
    I am ashamed,
    not of You,
    but of me.

I gloss up,
    but inside,

I feel caged
    by things
    I never
    wanted
    to touch.

I hold it all in:

    pain
    guilt
    shame

    the feeling of disappointment
    gnaws at me.
    Who can I blame but me?
    I took that path
    and now I don't know
    how to come
    to You.

The closer I get

the dirtier I feel.
The closer I get
the more
unworthy I feel.
The closer I get
the more I want
to pull away.

So, how do I come to sit in Your lap
    and let You hold me as I am

                            unclean and broken?

    How do I look at You

    Then at me and not feel hurt
    that there is not any resemblance of You in me?

I don't know how to return.

I CHOSE YOU, but I never called you "perfect."

I never called you "spotless"
I never labeled you "sinless."

My Child, you cannot hide you from me.
I let you go at your pace but I am never too far away.
I have been waiting to hear from you again.
I miss the way you checked-in.
I miss the time you came to me for advice.
You never have to fear I will cast you out.

My arms are
    always
    open.

I know the marks on your inner thigh.
    I know you self-inflicted them to redirect from the pain caused
by trespassers.

You are still beautiful to me.

I know you feel unworthy to come back to me.
    I know the bruises left on your neck reminds you of the years you
gave to them

— they were never built for you.

I know coming back to me isn't easy.

I know coming back to me seems like strangers meeting for
the first time.
But you are no stranger to me.

> *you are no foreigner to me.*

I know you.
I chose you.
I knew your heart before you knew
how to express it.
I knew you'd experience life.
I knew it all.

My arms are open

> *and ears attentive*
> *when you are ready.*

I want to know you from your heart not your mistakes.

COUNTLESS NIGHTS I drifted between tears

waiting
to
drown
me.

Meetings in my bedroom with the dark
    as it wrapped
    its arms
    around me.

Closed tabs,
    open tabs
    hoping for comfort
    only to be left in disgust.

Created playlists of
    what never should be remembered.

Everyone else moved
    and I remained stuck.
    I tried to smile and laugh
    but tears escaped.
    I tried productivity,
    eventually my body
    relived its trauma.

I've tried to comfort myself.

Orchestrated a soothing playlist
bathed in candles
bought comfort.
Escaped through a window seat
benched press to failure
concealed my face.

Tried to be my own support.
    I tried to take up less space.

I watched my breathing.
    Counted how many times
    I cried for help.

Found solace in
    what three dollars or
    thirty-five dollars could
    buy me in a night.

Created my own peace with a stench.
    Created safety within a man,
    a few of them.

I finally had control.

I finally had the power
    though
    it was none
    in my

. . .

"no."

I thought I had control.
    I thought I held the reins,
    but all I held was the weight of my own emptiness.

The comfort was fleeting,
    like smoke in the air,
    leaving me with nothing but ashes
    and the scent of defeat.

I was chasing something,
    someone,
    anything
    that might fill the hollow spaces
    within me.

But what I found was always
    temporary.
    What I found was never enough.

I tried to heal myself
    with things that could never heal,
    with distractions that only deepened the void.

I tried to comfort myself,
    but I was only running from the truth:

I needed You.

And yet, even as I write these words,
    there's fear.
    Fear that I've gone too far,
    that You'll look at me
    and see nothing but the mess I've made,
    the emptiness I've filled with distractions.

But still, I reach out.
    Still, I hope.
    Even when I've tried everything else,
    I'm here,
    waiting for something more.

I SAW THAT NIGHT—YOUR tears caught Our attention.

> *I felt the pain when you screamed, but I waited at the door.*
> *I remained outside the door. You like your privacy.*

>> *Your tears weren't wasted but they*
>> *needed to flow that night.*
>> *You harbored them in for so long,*
>> *you became weighted.*

I sent in the puppy to cling to you until you were ready for me. You need someone or something to see you when you didn't want to be seen. I knew you needed it for your safety. You started to smile again.

Would you believe me if I told you I sent Them out before you when you traveled?

>> *I sent Them out every night you took that drive to the overlook.*
>> *They waited on the ledge just in case.*
>> *They waited in the car three spaces down*
>> *just in case you let off the brakes.*

I always had a way out nearby.

>> *I know you never understood how you made it back home*
>> *those nights, half-sleep and barely sober.*
>> *I sent Them to help you on your travels. Do you remember*

*when you dozed and woke up to a red light? You closed your
eyes mid drift in traffic at a four-way intersection.*

I can be overprotective at times,

> *and I know you needed to feel control*

> *so I remained behind the scenes. Forgive me?*

I know it stopped working — all your remedies.
> *I know they stopped having any impact on you.*
> *I know the high wore off quicker than in the beginning.*
> *I know the drinks enhanced your emotions more than subdue
them.*
> *I know them holding you did nothing but make you nauseous.*
> *I know this conversation is hard for you to withstand.*

If it isn't too much to ask now,

can I have
> *a real chance?*

COMFORT WRAPPED in doubt
    is all I ever felt.
    From people with good intentions
    but too distant to know
    the depth of what I needed,
    the depth of the void.

They sat for a while
    until the darkness became too much,
    until the darkness became too heavy,
    until the darkness became too loud.

They got up and left.
    They left in hopes
    a short moment of comfort
    was enough.

They never waited it out,
    they never took me with them,
    they never asked me to come.

    They knew, what I knew,
    I was becoming too much.

The concept of comfort scares me.

I've experienced it once
    and it turned into grief.
    I don't actually like being alone
    but alone feels safe.

    I feel peace.

It's a space where my guard
    does not have to work overtime.
    My nerves get to rest.
    My body can exist.

I can be.

But You want me to be in good company
    and I don't even
    trust the good in me.

So, how do I trust the "good"—if any—in them?

What is good other than You?
    You want me to let them in?
    Let them close to me?
    Let them be around while I am broken?
    Let them see me cry?

Let them see me hurt?
Let them see me?

What if they don't stay?
   What if they get up and leave?
   What if they bring volume
   to what I have been muting?
   What if they aren't really for me?

You want me to take that risk?

Haven't I taken that risk enough?
   Haven't I given the benefit of the doubt enough?

Do You not see
   I've poured all I had left?
   I gave when it left me poor.

Is comfort worth it?

                         The risk?

TRUST

Me.

TRUST?
   It doesn't come that simple for me.
   I know what You've done for them,
   but its me.

I don't always feel
   like my requests matter
   that much to You.

I don't always feel
   like I am able to make those requests
   that everyone else makes.

I know Your word is true,
   and I feel they are not truly for me yet.

I know to pray without ceasing.
   I know to fast for breakthrough,
   but my prayers haven't seemed to be reaching You.

My fast has felt more
   like a hunger strike
   than catching Your attention.

I read Your words
   contradicting as they sometimes seem,
   I still chose to believe.

                    .   .   .

But that night happened
    and I never felt Your relief.
    That moment came
    and You watched me bleed.
    How do I trust You when I am not sure
    your actions will match what I need?

MY WORD WILL NEVER LIE to you,
  but you cannot put a timestamp on what I should do.
  You look to me as a genie but I am not here to grant your every
wish.
  A good father doesn't give their child every thing they desire
because somethings you desire will destroy you.

My words will only hold weight if you believe them.
  Believing is easy when your belief isn't put to the test.
  Believing doesn't come with a shield from suffering.
  I could never promise you that.
  Believing comes with reassurance.
  Believing isn't going to stop your storms from coming,
  but bring you peace amongst the turbulence.

You blame me for not showing up,
  when you ignored me warning you to never go.

You said
  you wanted
  control.

It feels like I'm taking up too much space.
    I "knew better."
    So I wait.
    I wait quietly and endure patiently
    because isn't this my payment,
    isn't this my reward?

The audacity of me to come to You
    knowing
    I am not ready.
    To come to You knowing
    I still want to go back
    though back ain't good for me.

THE FIRST TIME you tried to stand up
you fell back down.
You tried again
and fell back down.

The first time you tried to walk
you fell down.
You tried again
and you fell back down.

You may never be ready,
but keep coming.

One day you will be.

I FEEL like I am waiting to exhale
    and no one actually knows
    I've inhaled deadly toxins.

I've grown to enjoy this cycle.
    The inhale almost brings relief,
    but then I think of You.

I think of seeing You
    and chills chase down my spine.
    I think of seeing You
    and my heart beats to a new sound.
    I think of You
    and my knees kiss the ground
    and my head is no longer high
    and my lips moan unknown sounds
    and I feel covered.

"This presence is like no other."

I want to trust You,
    yet the undoing is scarier than
    the original experience
    itself.

I'll lean in.

I'll lean in with
    all of my curiosity,
    but promise me
    You will not think less of me?

Promise me,
    it will not cause
    You to not want me.

I HAVE grace
set aside
for you.

I DOUBT how much of
  a Father You really can be to me.
  You say You're a father to me,
  but what father sits back and
  watches His child suffer and not intervene?

You say You care about me,
  but Your care feels more like
  watching
  me
  break.

I DO NOT WATCH in pleasure.
  I am not silent as punishment.

You say you want me,
  but you want me in the way you desire.
  You want me to adapt to your needs
  and not come how I asked.
  You want to demand of me
  what you won't let me demand of you.

You want to be Abba and not child.
  I cannot do what you will not allow me the space to do.
  I cannot fix what you won't allow me to take.

I HAVE ALWAYS HAD MYSELF.
   I have always protected myself.

I don't know how
      to let someone else do it.
      I thought I was letting
      You do it.
      I thought I did
      let You lead.

To follow does that
      mean I do nothing?
      To follow does that
      mean I have no say?

I NEVER TOLD you to have yourself.
    I never expected you to be your own protection.

You assumed the role and never considered me.
    I've wanted to guide, protect, and lead you.
    I've desired to cover you.

I still do.

I ask you to follow behind
    not in silence
    but in trust.
    I want you to follow me
    not lead.

I WANT to feel safe with You,
   but safety feels like a language I've forgotten
   —or never really knew.

I never really wanted to lead.
   It was forced onto me.
   No one cared for me
   where I can rest
   and follow with assurance.
   No one wanted to lead me.

How can me leading myself
   be my fault?
   Why am I punished for doing
   what no one else would for me?

You made do with what
you knew.
I am not upset
at you.

The fear of punishment
is the awakened
knowledge of truth.

You know now what you
did not know then.

I NOW KNOW what
    I did not know then.

And knowing makes
    me feel guilt.
    It makes me feel dirty.
    It makes me feel unworthy.

I hated this world
    and prayed for an opt-out.
    I hated my situation
    and used anything
    to make me forget it.

I never chose You.
    I never came to You.
    Forgive me,
    I did not fully know.

I KNOW you've attempted many times
  and never succeeded.
   Tried to force a new pain
   to replace the pain that sits in your chest
   to replace the pain that keeps you up at night
   to replace the pain that feels like a weighted vest.

That isn't my will for you.
  It's not the plan for
  how your story will end.

I want you.
  I called you.
  I chose you.

Your life has greater purpose.
  What you knew isn't in question.

What do you believe about me?

  What do you believe in your heart about me?

I believe You are trustworthy.

Though I may not always understand,

I think You have my best in mind.

I trust You to protect me.

maybe not fully.
I know You have capabilities,
but You protect me after the deed is done.
You protect me not from the harm,
but from the residue trying to un-alive me.
I don't know which is better or which is worse.

I trust You to love me.

To see my defiled spirit and still call me Yours.

To search my heart and know corners are painted in hate
and pain, but still look at me and say "I love you,
anyways."

I don't know if that love is felt anywhere else.

You don't filter me but take me in totality.

The bad and the good.

The hope and the doubt.
The trauma and the forgiven parts.

PROTECTION DOESN'T ALWAYS COME in the format you prefer.

It will not always feel like safety in the moment.
It can feel like the stopping of an event.

It can feel like someone walking in to

cause awareness.
It can feel like me tearing a person away from you
because in their heart is hatred of you.

My protection doesn't come looking like Prince Charming,
    but when it comes,
    it comes to guard you in the moment of
    your sorrow

        your betrayal

            your heartbreak

I protect you
    but I cannot shield you
    from all.
    I protect you
    but I cannot keep
    you aloof
    to the realities
    of being away from me.

YOU TOOK HER FROM ME!
   YOU TOOK HER.
   WHY DID YOU TAKE HER!
   WHY DIDN'T YOU
   HEAL HER!?

YOU BROKE MY
   FAMILY.
   YOU CAUSED THEM
   PAIN.
   YOU SAID IF
   WE PRAYED
   IN YOUR SON'S NAME
   YOU WILL HONOR IT.

WHY DIDN'T YOU HONOR IT?
   WHY DIDN'T YOU KEEP YOUR WORD?

GIVE HER BACK TO ME.
   BRING HER BACK.
   PLEASE.

bring her back.

I prayed to You in Your son's name
    and You still took her.

I fasted for healing
    and You ignored me.

I cried at Your feet because
    You are supposed to be close to
    the broken-hearted
    and You looked
    away
    from me.

But You want me
    to trust You,
    how?

Was my brokenness too much for You to see?
    Did You not consider how much it is for me to feel it?
    The shattering at every moment I think "I'm okay."
    The grief that sits in my throat eager to
    be released at the words
    "Are you really okay?"

But You knew all of this was going to happen.
    You knew I couldn't go high on a building

        and You not find me.

You knew I couldn't run and hide in the darkest room

and You not find me.

You knew I couldn't drive fast enough

and You be away from me.

So I stayed put.
I stayed in faith.

I prayed,

I fasted,

and You were mute.

Why didn't You
answer me?
Why?

I hear her voice every time I lay down.
    I see her caramel complexion
    when I look in the mirror.

I smell her cashmere scent in the spice aisle.
    You took her and left me to grieve
    with questions lingering.

You took her before
    I became fruitful.
    You took her though
    I prayed in Your sons' name.

I'M NOT TRYING to hurt you.
    I'm not intentionally trying to cause you pain.

But you have to face
    what was to be able to
    receive what should be.

YOU LET me experience grief often.

I begin to expect it quarterly.

I rehearse my scream for when they tell me
or I see.

I coach myself.

"Breathe."

"You have to breathe."

"Calm down."

"Come on. You have to
exhale."

"In"

"Out."

"Breathe."

I rehearse my lines when un-aliving myself wants to become my only option.

"You have to remain strong."

"God is close to you… believe it."

"If you give up, how will they believe He is real?"

"Fight."

"He let you borrow them."

"Fight."

"He isn't punishing you.

"Fight."

"He still cares for you."

"Fight."

"Breathe."

"Fight."

"Endure and fight."

Shattered glass

    the theme song to this season.

        I replay visions of driving

                being t-boned on
                    the side

      headlights mimic the idea of heaven.

I see me.

    Bloody.
    Tears pigmented pink.
    Arms shaking but I feel

          no pain.

I experience this daily.

    Grief never ceases to exist.

        The losses hold weight in my gut

   my chest and mind become pinball

        bouncing memories and sounds

              pinging pain and happiness.

I shouldn't have to experience this.

FIND ME IN THE LOSS.
Come to me and let me bear your grief.
I don't "take" to cause you more pain but to show you even in sorrow I am there.
Even in unexpected losses I am good.

I know it hurts.
I know you wanted them here.

But can I not fill that emptiness?

Can I be enough to stand in the gap?

Give me a chance.

Just one chance.

Let me prove to you who I am. Let Me show you who your grandparents spoke to you about.

Encounter Me.
Un-harden your heart towards Me.
Let Me show you the good in grief.

Let Me show you the beauty in the ashes.

Let Me show you there is always more life in death.

THE REQUEST You make are huge.
   You make a request knowing I'm on edge.

   You make requests knowing I already feel like I have
   nothing left to lose.

                    But, why me?

   Why are You allowing me to be hurt in the first place?

   Why the constant pain?

   Once I am healed from one thing,

   You allow another thing to break me again.
   You allow another thing to discourage me.
   You leave me sitting in a pit of sorrow.

   What have I done to You?

   I've loved You. I've spoken about You. I haven't forsaken Your
                         name.

I've followed all the rules.
   I've served.
   I've sowed.
   I've prayed.
   I've gave.

And where has it left me?

When are You going to rescue me from this?

When are You going to part my Red Sea?

Can't You see I'm tired.

I have no more fight left in me.

You're just watching me.
Are You happy to see me
broken?
Happy to see me hurt?
You're supposed to be a Father,
What kind of Father lets their
child suffer?
What kind of Father ignores
their child's cry?

A good Father doesn't do that.

IF I RESCUE you every time you feel the heat, what would you learn?

If I step in at every word said that you did not like, what would you learn?

If I covered you from pain and hurt, would you appreciate life?

I am not a Father happy when you are hurt, but I rejoice because it all is going to work for your good.

I am not a Father ignoring your cry, but I am wiping your tears, while you learn to stay in communion with me.

Breathe.

Breathe.

Breathe.

I have never left you to bear alone.
But think back.
Back to your first encounter of pain.

You respond to it differently now.

You don't lose balance like that first moment.

Now what if
I stopped it?
If I took that hit
for you.

HIS BELOVED

I am shielding you but I need you to experience the world so you fully know Me.

How much more are You asking me to endure?

How much more do I have to encounter before
I am at peace?

I will give you peace

in

the midst
of the
storm.

THE DAYS ARE BECOMING EASIER for me.

How are You so patient?
How are You so willing to continue
to remain when my first thought is always to escape?
Do You ever want to turn Your back on me?
Do You ever want to just walk away
and find someone more willing?

Am I really the type of child You want?

A GOOD FATHER understands the change in seasons.

    Seasons happen in cycles and when you can pay attention to their arrival, departure, and coming, you learn to be content with the shifts.

The changes you experience are not great enough for me to abort you.

    I will not disown you.

                  I know your words come

    from a place of

    emotion,
    so I come sound.

When you first made it known
    you existed within your mother,
    My world brightened.
    My joy increased.

You gave your mother so much pain during those months,
    but I knew it was because you were a fighter.

You could've walked away from Me years ago.

    But you stayed.

                  You had more to say to me.

I hope you always have
more to say to Me.

YOU CALL ME A FIGHTER, but I feel like I am constantly losing these battles. My mother told me once, "you are not fighting against what you see."

> It never made sense.
> How do I fight if I cannot see my opponent?
> How do I have a chance to win if I am already
> at a disadvantage?

YOU NEVER WERE AT A DISADVANTAGE.
   You've always had the upper hand.
   You fight not through your natural eyes,
   you've been fighting since
   you've been at my feet.

Your prayers dispatched Us on your behalf.
   You may not see now,
   but the time is coming
   when the veil will be broken.

I FEEL SO WEAK, though.

I feel burdened by a fight I never asked to be in.
Why did You enlist me?
Why did You draw my name?

I just need a break.
I am tired of fighting.
I am tired of enduring.
I am tired.

When is my rest coming?

When is mine?

LET ME FIGHT FOR YOU.

If I tell you rest, will you listen?

My intent isn't for you to be weighed down, but I need you to trust Me.

Give Me a little trust the size of a mustard seed.

Rest in this storm, while I handle the matter.

I see what is coming,
but you won't stand behind Me.

Let Me be Father for you.

Let Me be the Father you cried for in the night.

Let Me be the Father you wish stayed and didn't walk away.

Let Me be the Father who loves you enough to put their own life on the line.

Yes, you are worth all of that to Me.

How do I let You?
I cannot let You.
I am unworthy of a Father like You.
What makes me so deserving of a selfless love?

You see what I've done.

I walked away from You.

I cursed your name out of pain.

I never said "sorry."

So, why should I be given Your warm embrace?

There was a night I prayed about this moment. So many hypotheticals—practicing my lines and anticipating Yours. I was ready to make my case. I was ready to stand my ground. I was ready to fight to prove my actions were justified. I rehearsed my tone and posture when I was to see You face to face.

A hypothetical was never Your love.
A hypothetical was never Your forgiveness.

This Abba, I want to rest.

I want to be in peace.

I have never felt worthy of this life.
Why did You choose me?
Why did You continue to choose me?
I've gone astray desiring only my way.

I don't know how to find my way back to You
    — not really.
    But if You're still calling me Your child,
    help me believe it.

Hold me, even when I push You away.
    Love me, even when I doubt You.
    Teach me how to rest in Your arms again.

"I want to go home."

My Reflection

I ALWAYS DESIRED an open conversation with my dad. It was never anything on his part that stopped the conversation from happening. We spent many nights watching the Fast & Furious series and 24. I'd tag-along on Saturdays to wash the car, grab coffee, check the P.O. Box, and grab lunch. We spent time together. Sitting with my dad was enough growing up. I took pride in people saying, "You look just like your dad." The resemblance of him whenever I went places without him gave me joy. I am a daddy's girl, but I am the daddy's girl that's more fearful of disappointing him than anything else.

I've had the pleasure of watching my dad up close and personal. My dad isn't just my dad but also my pastor. The weight of ministry often meant sitting on a pedestal within limitations. A fear of slight mistakes rung in the back of my mind constantly. The older I became, the more I realized I needed my dad in a different capacity. The barrier stopping me wasn't his unavailability, but it was my fear of taking up too much space and burdening him with my woes. My dad is not shut off to talking, I just struggled with being vulnerable. Vulnerability, for me, meant admitting the weight of life, ministry, and being was getting to me. It was admitting the pressure was becoming too much to bear. It was admitting I wanted an out from it all. Even writing these words now causes an ache in my chest but all of these things were what I desired to tell my dad. I hesitated to be vulnerable with him because I did not want him to think he did anything wrong when raising me. I cared more about how my honesty would effect him than freeing myself and requesting the help, wisdom, protection, and comfort I desired deeply.

ABBA: FATHER, I WILL OBEY YOU.

Our hesitation in looking to God as our Father is often rooted in our comparison to our earthly fathers. We compare a perfect God to our earthly fathers who are limited by flesh. Our earthly fathers who were present and active, or may have left and abandoned us, we place that same lens on the perfect God. We expect God to be like our earthly father, who gave us everything without ever telling us "no." A earthly father believing that their child should have the world by any means, so when God tells us "no" or "wait," we view him as incapable or cruel.

We expect God to be like our earthly father working multiple jobs to ensure we are taken care of but missing every important event because of those same jobs. An earthly father upholding the title of provider but not understanding our love language is quality time and affirmations. So when we come to God, it is hard to fathom he can be all we want and all we need.

And sometimes we are slow to trust bringing everything to God because everything is wrapped in confusion, too. We are confused and conflicted by how we feel. We know God is all-knowing and righteous, but at the same time, we do not understand how an all-knowing God still wants us to come to explain the pain He knows we already feel. Or, we are confused, with questions our leaders, family, and friends, cannot seem to give us answers to, so if they are unable to untangle our confusion and if God is not a god of confusion then who is left to listen to us as we think aloud?

Accepting God the Father is dependent on understanding God is the original father. That, no offense to your good dad, no other father on earth could ever compare. Our confusion does not cause God to shut us down and push us away. Our questions do not cause God to go mute on us. Our desire for connection is not ignored by objects of our desire. God the father loves us individually and collectively. The one and only God can be a provider and comforter towards us. He can discipline us and still be good and want the best for us. And the good news: He can and He is.

God is not the reflection of our earthly fathers, he is the perfection of our earthly father. God is everything we wanted our earthly fathers to be. God is the provider that will never miss a moment to be with us. God is the protector that will never push us away for mistakes we created. God is the perfect listener that will not judge our pain though self-inflicted.

God is waiting with open arms and attentive ears, will you come?

Yeshua

Yeshua (יֵשׁוּעַ) is the original Hebrew name of **Jesus**, meaning **"Yahweh is salvation."** A shortened form of *Yehoshua*, it reflects His divine mission to save and redeem. Commonly used in Messianic and Hebrew-rooted Christian traditions, *Yeshua* connects believers to the rich heritage of biblical faith.

I CAN'T CARRY another day like this.
    In just a few fleeting moments,
    everything unraveled—
    chaos crept in,
    and nothing feels steady anymore.

Place me back on Your wheel.
    Shape me.
    Mold me.
    Position me back in Your will.
    Right now.

I can't keep moving like this.
    In just a few days, chaos erupted—
    everything I held steady slipped out of place.
    Put me back on Your wheel,
    reshape me in Your will,
    realign me to Your purpose.

Right now, all I can do is listen.
    No more prophecies.
    No more distant promises of blessings.
    I need You to move.
    Pull me out of this pit.
    Please, pull me out.

I decree and declare:
    I am healed.
    I am whole.
    I have peace.
    I have power.

(Repeat it until my spirit believes it.)

I am healed.
    I am whole.
    I have peace.
    I have power.

They call You Savior,
    Redeemer,
    Friend,
    but I don't always know what that means.
    I've heard of Your love,
    but some days I feel so unworthy of it.
    I wonder if You see me,
    if You know what it's like to feel this broken

                              to feel this lost
                              to feel this alone.

Do You see me?
    When I call on Your name,
    do You hear me,
    or am I whispering into the void?
    They say You are near to the brokenhearted,
    but I've sat in the dark for so long,
    wondering if I've broken too much for You to stay.

I am here.

You're the perfection of our kind
 —the guide for our life
 You got it all right.
 No blemish defiles You.
 No lie discredits You.
 You stand perfect and true.
 You stood meek and selfless.

But did You ever want to?
 Were your desires considered?

When I first heard about You
 my heart ached.
 You came to handle Your Father's business, and Your Father's business left You in a difficult position.

He sent You on a suicide mission. Are You mad at him? Do You resent him? I never could understand a father willing to send their only child, and their boy at that.

He sent You here knowing You'd be misunderstood

 knowing You'd be hated,

 knowing You'd be lied on,

 knowing You'd be betrayed.

But He still sent You.

His

perfect son,
His

only son.

Does that hurt You

knowing the purpose of Your life is to be the One?

TREES PROVIDE shade for weary travelers on the road.
Bees provide honey to sweeten a meal.
Clouds provide rain to water the fields.
The sun provides light.
The wind provides a breeze on a hot day.
The sheep provides a warm robe.
The lamb provides substance for a family.

Every thing has a purpose that must be fulfilled.

Purpose is heavy for some and lighter for others.
Purpose can be misunderstood, too.

If I didn't go, then I'd have caused a blockage for you.

CAN we be real with each other?

Obedience is sometimes the sacrifice,

or at least, it requires one.

Our Father said its better to obey, but obeying isn't

always logical for me.

I obey and still lose something.
I obey and still feel alone.
I obey and still lack provisions.
I obey and still have no clarity.
I obey and still hurt.
I obey and still am betrayed.

I obeyed for a long time, but why did it feel as though my obedience continually came at the expense of me? Every time I obeyed, something was taken away.

It feels like it came at the price of my desires.

Help me understand the purpose in obedience if no immediate gain. Help me understand the purpose in obedience if I never will see the reward.

LOOK INWARD.
Do you obey out of awe or out of mandate?
Do you obey out of resentment or pure joy?

I obeyed with tears in my eyes,
but fulfillment in my heart.
I submitted to the call
though it left me misunderstood
and betrayed.

Why do you submit?

I'M SUPPOSED TO, *right?*

I am supposed to lay my life down.
Isn't Christian synonymous with surrender?
Does it really matter if I want to or not?
Does if I agree change the fact that submission is a
prerequisite?

Don't get me wrong I submit because I am supposed to,
but I submit because I really don't know.
I don't have knowledge of my future.
I don't have insight to lead my own life.
I barely know what to wear the next day.
I barely know what I want to eat,

let alone if I am really hungry or bored.

I submit because it takes a weight off of me, most times but
not always.
I like control, but if I am honest, it makes me anxious.
The weight of being in control leaves all the decision

making on me and I know I fall short.

I know I lack in some areas. I know I am mere man. So giving
up some of that control is fine with me. I don't want it all. To be
like a child with little worries and responsibilities is all I want. But
child submission and child of God submission is different.

A child of God submits at a lowly place. Having to constantly
admit dependence no matter how many degrees I obtain or
awards I receive. I'm always still back on my knees. The path
wasn't as narrow at first. First, I was stripped of things never
attached to me.

I let go the drinking because I need to be sober in your sight.
I gave up the crop tops and revealing shirts to remain modest.

WHEN I CAME I knew my life was one of surrendering.
*I knew submission meant I would have to believe and trust in
the mission of our Father.*
I surrendered my life for His glory
but I will not tell you it will be easy.

This journey does not always come with an itinerary.
It comes with principles to practice,
*but no precursor on when or how long you'll be in practice before
game time.*

My itinerary was joyful at times.
I met people like you and made friends.
Other times, I realized the cost of surrendering
and had to ponder on that.
I had to understand "the one for the many"
is the way and will of the Father.

Do You ever get tired..

of the cutting..

and the bleeding...

The pain You never asked to endure.

Do You ever want to curse them?
 Plead the fifth to spare Yourself?
 I do. I hate being the one for the many.
 Teacher, I cannot be like You.
 The cutting feels deep and personal and never-ending.

Before I couldn't go without reverencing Him.
    I needed to remain as close as possible.
    I wanted to be near because near felt safe.
    Near felt righteous.
    Near felt whole.
    Near felt beautiful.
    Near felt peaceful.

But I slowed down my pace.

    Near began to require much of me.
    I wanted explanations, but never asked.
    Eventually, I wandered and took the scenic route.

        I was in awe, but this route left me

worse than how I came.

        So, I tried to return,
       but my heart wasn't fully
        ready to give
          in.

I never lost sight, but I added a few stops on the journey.
    I desired to enjoy life
    because proximity
    was
    a
    tight
    leash.

        . . .

I think I understand now, though.
    If I could go back, I would.
    If I knew what I knew now, I'd remain glued to His hip.

Friend, I messed up.

I'm still here.

THIS WAS the year of extraction,
    a tearing away of who I was.

It hurts.
    This breaking, this remaking—
    it came not with grace,
    but with force.
    Change after change, week after week,
    I can barely recognize myself.

You're shaping me, I think,
    into who I was always meant to be,
    but it hasn't been gentle.
    It hasn't been patient.
    It's been forceful—
    and it hurts.

Mismatched and forced in
    only to be removed.

I admit I took on Your role
    not realizing the weight every decision held,
    not understanding beginning from ending.
    Like Job, I questioned Your management.

I've tried to keep up,
    tried to follow where You lead,
    but I can't seem to find my footing.
    I can't catch hold of You

long enough to steady myself,
long enough to keep moving forward.

My endurance is fading,
    carry me.

THIS WALK WAS NEVER MEANT to be easy.
This year has felt like an extraction
because that is the cost.

If I let you keep it all,
you'd grow to believe that's all
you had, all you'd ever need.

You would think
what you had was the best
I had for you.

BUT I WAS CONTENT.
  I wasn't searching for more,
  wasn't reaching for anything else.
  I had settled into a quiet rhythm,
  a stillness I thought was enough.

I wasn't restless.
  I wasn't desperate.

I didn't ask for change.
  I didn't ask to be uprooted.
  I didn't ask for my world to shift
  like sand beneath my feet.

I was okay—
  or at least, I thought I was.
  But somehow, even in my contentment,
  something stirred.
  Something cracked open.
  And now I'm here,
  caught between what was
  and whatever it is You're doing.

WERE YOU TRULY OKAY,
or were you just afraid to ask for more?
Was your faith only bold enough
to reach for what felt within your grasp,
even without My help?

You said you didn't need anything else,
but what you held onto
was so much less than what I had for you.

You settled—
content with shadows of promises,
content with fragments of joy,
content with a life far below
what We dreamed for you.

You grew comfortable in spaces
never designed to hold you,
satisfied with the bare minimum,
as if you aren't woven into Us,
as if you aren't part of something
infinitely greater.

I DIDN'T HAVE the faith—
    I'll admit it.

I didn't ask for what my heart truly longed for,
    because asking and being met with silence
    hurts far more than staying quiet.

I didn't have the courage to reach beyond
    what was already in my hands,
    because deep down,
    I don't always feel worthy of holding more.

It's easier to settle in smallness
    than to risk the weight of disappointment.

I am still new to this—
    being seen.

Not just glanced at, not just noticed,
    but truly seen.
    Eyes meeting mine,
    peering past the walls I've built,
    past the rehearsed smiles
    and carefully curated words.

I'm not used to standing still under this light.
    I've spent so long hiding in shadows,
    shrinking myself down to fit into spaces
    never meant to hold me.

Being seen feels vulnerable,
    like standing in the middle of an open field
    with no armor, no shield,
    just me—raw and exposed.

It feels like an invitation and a risk
    all at once.

What if I'm seen and rejected?
    What if I'm seen and deemed unworthy?
    What if being seen means being misunderstood?

AND WHAT IF...
   being seen is where you finally exhale?
   What if being seen is where love meets you?
   What if being seen is where healing begins?
   What if being seen is knowing Me?

I'M STILL LEARNING how to stay here,
    to let myself be fully visible,
    to trust that You see me—
    not just the polished parts,
    not just the pieces I'm proud of,
    but the trembling hands, the tear-streaked face,
    the soaked cuffs of my hoodies,
    the questions, the doubts, the fears.

I'm still new to this,
    but I want to stay.
    Even if it's uncomfortable,
    even if it's messy,
    I want to stay.

THEN STAY.
   Stay here with Me.

WHEN YOU WENT OFF ALONE
    did You really go to pray?
    Or did You need privacy
    because no one felt safe?
    Did You hide in plain sight
    because You knew what you'd have to face
    and You could not show them how
    afraid You were?

Being alone feels safe for me.
    Guards are down,
    the masquerade is over.
    Is that the secret place?

WHEN I WENT OFF ALONE,
  yes, I prayed—
  but I also exhaled.

I let the weight fall from My shoulders,
  even if just for a moment.
  Not because My Father wasn't near in the crowd,
  but because solitude made it easier to hear Him.

Did I need privacy? Yes.
  Not because I was hiding from them,
  but because I was holding so much
  they couldn't understand.
  They couldn't see the full picture.
  They couldn't feel the weight of eternity
  pressing against every choice I made.

I wasn't hiding out of fear—
  I was retreating to remain steady.

You ask if I was afraid.
  I'll tell you this:
  I felt the tremor in My hands,
  the knot in My chest,
  the quiet ache of knowing what was ahead.
  But fear never held Me back.
  It pushed Me closer to My Father, Our Father.

Being alone does feel safe, doesn't it?
  The walls can fall,

99

the tears can come,
the questions can spill out without judgment.
But solitude isn't meant to be an escape forever.
It's meant to be a secret place—
a refuge, not a retreat.
A space to meet the Father,
to steady your heart,
to gather strength before stepping back out.

When you're there, let your guards down.
Drop the mask.
Let the silence speak louder than your fears.
Because in the secret place,
you'll find Me there too.

So You're human?

FULLY.

AND, You're God?

FULLY.

Did You ever see them as selfish?
    Did You ever feel like a thing,
    an object to be used,
    instead of a person to be loved?

Did You ever want to walk away—
    to call it quits,
    to tell Your Father,
    "I can't do this.
    Not at my life's expense"?

Why is it always the One for the many?
    Does no one care how the One feels?
    Why must the One always be the sacrifice,
    the One to carry the unbearable weight?

No one ever asks about the torment,
    the burden You never chose,
    yet it clung to You like a shadow—
    always present,
    keeping pace as You ran,
    finding comfort in the dark
    just as it did in the light.

Did You ever question the purpose of Your life?
    Did You ever wonder why such a heavy mantle
    had to be placed on You?
    Did You ever wish You could just be... normal?
    Live a quiet life,
    hidden, unnoticed,
    moving below the radar?

Did You ever wrestle with it all,
    knowing how it would end for You?
    Do You ever regret it?

If You had the choice again,
    would You have come down?

Was I worth it to You?

Why does it seem like, to everyone else,
    I'm just an afterthought?
    I consider them, I bend for their needs,
    even when it costs my own joy—
    but nobody does the same for me.

Nobody notices, nobody sees.
    It's always "thank you"
    when I'm no longer there to hear it.
    It sucks. It hurts.
    What am I doing wrong?
    Am I the problem?

One year gone, and all I hear is,
    "I was distracted."
    One whole year—
    reduced to "we made it to a year."
    Am I not worth being fought for?
    Am I not worth being cherished?

Help me to give like You did.
    To pour out without keeping score,
    to love without resentment.
    But it's hard—
    because I feel like everyone takes from me,
    emptying me,
    leaving me hollow.

Do they see how tired I am?
    Do they see how drained I've become?
    Or am I just a well to be drawn from,

until there's nothing left?

How did You endure it?
    How did You love them,
    knowing they would leave You?
    Teach me to give without breaking,
    to love without losing myself.

Are they God or Am I?
Child, you keep holding their words with so much weight
because of their titles and age,
and you've created a habit of taking everyone else's word
about you over My Word about you.

There can only sit one person on this throne of your life.
But I am not going to keep telling you to move.
You wanted me to save you,
and I am trying to.
You asked me to bring you peace,
I am trying to.
Joseph couldn't help anyone while at home until he left.
Ruth couldn't help anyone at home until she left.

Obedience is hard now, but it strengthens your faith if you let it.

WHY DOES obedience have to feel like a battle?
   Why can't You just shape my thoughts
   to align with Yours?
   Why not open my eyes
   so I see things the way You do?

Why not just make me submit?
   Force my will into Yours,
   bend my stubborn heart
   until it stops resisting.

Please, bend it.

Because right now,
   it feels like my flesh is winning—
   over and over again.
   I know the war is raging inside me,
   but I'm so tired of losing.

I keep losing. I keep fighting
   and I cannot seem to overcome this.

If You want me to follow,
   why not make the path easier?
   Why let me stumble so much?
   Why let me wrestle when You could just speak,
   and I'd obey?

IF I MADE OBEDIENCE EFFORTLESS,
would it still be love?
Would it still be trust?
Or would it just be control?

I could have shaped your thoughts,
aligned your vision,
and bent your will to Mine—
but then you'd just be a puppet,
not My Beloved.

Obedience isn't just about the outcome;
it's about the intimacy formed in the choosing.
Every moment you wrestle and still turn toward Me,
you're saying, 'I trust You more than myself.'

I know it's hard.
I know your flesh feels loud,
your spirit feels faint,
and the war within you feels endless.
But each battle you face
shapes you into someone stronger,
someone more like Me.

You see loss in your stumbles,
but I see growth in every time you get back up.
I see love in every moment you try again.
I see trust in every whispered prayer
when you feel like giving up.

. . .

I'm not asking for perfection.
    I'm asking for your heart.
    Even in the mess.
    Even in the struggle.

So lean into Me when it feels impossible.
    When you feel like you're losing,
    know that I've already won.

"It is finished."

You built a circle of friends,
    knowing they'd never fully understand You.
    You carried truths they couldn't grasp,
    walked paths they couldn't follow.

You were changing—constantly, deeply—
    yet they rarely noticed.
    Did they see the shift in Your eyes?
    Did they feel the weight in Your silence?
    Did they sense the fire beneath Your calm exterior?

You weren't always the table-flipping friend.
    At first, You were the one who said,
    'Come as you are, and I'll love you there.'
    You were the steady presence,
    the unwavering voice,
    the one who gave without keeping score.

You were the emotionally stable friend,
    the selfless friend,
    the one who carried everyone else's burdens
    while quietly holding Your own.

    But even the strongest hands tremble.

Even the most patient hearts have limits.
    And I wonder—
    did they notice when the shift came?
    When righteous anger broke through kindness?
    When silence turned into confrontation?

I can only imagine the weight of being so deeply known,

yet still so deeply misunderstood.

The manipulation,
    the violation,
    the false accusation
    yet You remained silent.

How?
    Their words cut to a point of no return.
    Triggering a wound I hadn't unlearned.
    They mocked what took courage,
    and accused what they didn't understand.

I only ever wanted to be normal.

             Why can't I just fit in?

IF I LET you believe
you're cut from their cloth,
you'd inherit their limits,
their fears, their fate.

You'd settle—
content with their harvest,
never realizing the fruit I've grown for you
is set apart, chosen,
handpicked by Me.

Your roots are planted in different soil,
your branches stretched toward a different sky.
What I've prepared for you
can't be compared,
can't be measured
by what they've received.

You like to silence your calling
to match their volume.

Don't.

I'm torn.

Am I here to learn to be like You,
    or just to hear about You?
    The stories captivate me,
    but letting them sink in—letting them change me—
    feels like too much.
    Too raw. Too vulnerable.

Still, I recite Your words.
    I speak them with a love that trembles,
    with clarity, with conviction.
    I make them simple,
    yet they remain whole, untouched.

But to live them?
    To embody them for myself?
    That's different.
    That feels like stepping into the light,
    fully exposed, every flaw, every fracture—seen.

So tell me...
    What do I do with this?

THERE'S this woman I met by a well—
    carrying more than just her water jar.
    She hid behind words,
    behind glances cast downward,
    but her heart spoke louder
    than her silence ever could.

Shame trembled on her lips,
    embarrassment sat heavy on her shoulders,
    but light met her there—
    not to expose, but to heal.

Her chains loosened,
    her burden lifted,
    not because she hid herself,
    but because she let Me see her.

Let Me see you.

You know, I want to heal.

Like, really heal.
I want to heal but I don't know
where to begin.
I don't really know what to do.
I just know I'm not okay.

I smile, but the curves are met with tears.

      I breathe and every exhale is weighted.

I'm broken at the core. I despise my body for betraying
me and my

mind for being an accomplice.

The longevity of this lifestyle makes me lose hope.

      Why do You want to be called my friend?

IF YOU WERE MEANT to be perfect, I'd have no purpose here.
  If you were meant to be blameless, I'd have no purpose here.

I call you friend because the shame you feel I will help carry. The burden I want to help bear.
  A friend isn't there for the good times and then neglects you during the darkness.

  A friend isn't there for the celebrations and turns their back on the losses.

  A friend isn't there for new beginnings and not there to help with endings.

Your seasons aren't too much for me.

  I am not a seasonal friend.

Count on me.

DID You grieve alone for what was required of You?
Did the weight of being chosen
crush the solace You once knew?
Did You mourn the quiet places,
the familiar rhythms,
the fleeting comfort of a life You'd grown to love?

I've carved out a routine,
a fragile home in the patterns of my days.
Now I'm asked to leave it behind,
to unravel my comfort,
to step into the unknown
once more.

How did You do it?
You walked the earth with so little,
yet surely even You found shelter
in the small, steady things.
Didn't You know the taste of peace,
the softness of a moment You could trust?
Didn't You ache,
knowing even that would be taken?

You knew the end,
yet still, You stayed.
How did You bear the knowing?

Our Father is a father of pivots.

On my journey, I met many people I wanted to remain by my side.

I even friended a few.

Some couldn't handle the journey because there were questions I wasn't able to answer.

There was uncertainty in my walk with our Father.

Our Father had me pivot from the normal ways of this world.

A foreign way of life, huh?

But in remaining different from their ways, I found new comfort in knowing I was in His will.

Yes, I had moments where I could not speak on a matter.

Those moments were lonelier than a star in the sea of night.

But He comforted me.

He gave me reassurance in my purpose.

To say I didn't know is to say we aren't one.

I AM CONFUSED AND SCARED.
    I think I get it, and with the little I get,
    it feels like I am asking to be placed on the frontlines.
    I know I shouldn't be fearful,
    but I don't want to take anymore hits.
    I have wounds still open waiting to be seen.
    I have bruises festering
    and yet there is still an ask of me.

Forgive me.

"Forgive me."
    I look at me and complain,
    then I look at Your hands
    and feel pain.
    I look at Your head and see the trail of mockery left behind.
    Friend, I wish I could say I deserve You,
    but I am not worthy.

If I could've been there, I would've taken You down.
    I would've told them to take him instead.

Why do I feel rage when I think of it?
    They made a spectacle out of You.
    They make punchlines out of You,
    the One who provided
    them with access to eternal life.

Why are You a friend to them, too?

YOU DIDN'T ALWAYS SEE me as a friend.
  You saw me and felt pity.
  You saw me and felt sorrow.
  You saw me and felt empathy.

You didn't call me friend
  until you needed me.

They don't feel the need, yet.
  But I still will be here for them,
  like I was for you.

A good friend understands
  how to patiently wait through
  the process.

I am not here for a moment
  but eternity.

DOES that mean You are a friend to **them**, too?
    After all they did to me,
    You still want to be **their** friend?

What happened to light not associating with darkness?
    What happened to my table being prepared in front of my
enemies?
    What happened to avenging me?
    How is that fair?
    Where is their judgement?
    Where is their punishment?

That night I called out to You,
    and You still see a "good" in them?
    The words said about You, and You still
    want to give them a chance?

How can You be my friend and theirs?
    How can You want both of us?

I want You to not want them.
    I want You to choose me over them.
    I want them to hurt how I hurt.

Why does that
    make **me** the bad person?

You know... someone once felt this same ache.
They carried a hunger for justice,
a craving for judgment to fall on the one
who wounded them so deeply.

Their heart wouldn't soften,
their mind wouldn't let go.
They saw every event from their angle,
every moment as something done to them,
never with them.

But here's the thing:
What makes life so tangled, so wicked,
isn't just that people have free will—
it's that one person's free will
collides with another's.
It crashes.
It bruises.
It leaves marks neither intended to make.

But... what if I told you someone once prayed
that same desperate prayer—about you?
What if you were their villain?
What if, in their story, you were the one they begged God to
judge?

YET HERE YOU ARE—STILL loving.
Still forgiving.
Still carrying the weight they placed on Your shoulders.

How did You do it?
How did You hold both the title of villain and Savior
and still choose grace?

GRACE BECOMES
easier to choose
when you see it
as more gift
than burden.

You know, sometimes Grace feels like
    an unearned inhale after holding your breath for too long.
    It's like the pause between guilt and forgiveness,
    a bridge suspended over the chasm of shame.

It doesn't rush.
    It does not force or demand.
    It arrives—slow, soft, steady, and certain.

It's the warm light that spills into my darkness
    the steady whisper that says, "I still love you,"
    even when your hands are stained
    with the aftermath of your own choices.

It isn't fair, but it's good, I guess.
    It's never weighed scales or counted offenses.
    My perfection doesn't earn it,
    my failure doesn't revoke it.

It meets you in the middle—
    in the mess, in the wreckage,
    in the bitter taste of regret.

And somehow, without explaining itself,
    Grace lifts my chin, wipes my tears,
    and invites me to try again.

Grace sounds like You.

I Am.
> *Wrapped in flesh, walking among you.*
> *I didn't just talk about it; I had to become it.*
> *Every step I took, every word I spoke,*
> *was an invitation: "Come to Me."*

When others drew lines in the sand,
> *I crossed them.*
> *When they held stones in their hands,*
> *I stayed their grip.*
> *When they demanded justice,*
> *I offered mercy.*

I saw you—before you hid,
> *before you ran,*
> *before you believed the lie that you were too far gone.*
> *I saw you, and I stayed.*

On that cross, I stretched out My arms,
> *and I whispered through the pain:*
> *"It is finished."*

Every lash, every thorn, every nail—
> *I took them willingly.*
> *Not out of obligation, but love.*

You didn't have to earn this Grace.
> *You never could.*
> *But I gave it freely, fully, forever.*

. . .

I am not just the giver of Grace;
   I Am.

I USED to think Grace was a blanket
    to cover my mistakes.
    But now I see—it's a fire.
    One that purifies,
    refines, and sets my soul aglow.

Forgive me,
    for ever taking Your Grace lightly.
    Forgive me,
    for treating it like a safety net for my reckless choices.
    Help me see it as the lifeline it truly is.

I know Grace isn't deserved,
    but it's given.
    Freely.
    Over and over again.

And I am learning to breathe in that reality,
    to let it hold me steady,
    to let it carry me home.

UNCONDITIONAL. Unfailing. Unending.
   When you feel unworthy,
   when shame grips your throat,
   when the weight of your failures pulls you down—
   remember:
   I came for you.
   I stayed for you.
   I died for you.
   And I rose for you.

I am Grace, and I am here.
   I Am.

My Reflection

FRIENDSHIP IS a challenging space to navigate. In elementary school, it feels simple—making friends is as easy as checking a box or sharing a favorite color. By middle school, friendships become more territorial and possessive, marked by cliques and the fear of exclusion. High school adds another layer of complexity, where communication—or the lack of it—can make or break connections.

As we step into young adulthood, our lives shift. Our passions emerge, our priorities change, and we attempt to grow without realizing growth often requires more space—space for others, space for honesty, and space for vulnerability.

It's not until college or the early stages of adulthood that we realize lasting friendships demand more than shared interests or surface-level conversations. They require openness, trust, and the willingness to be seen—truly seen.

You must sit with the uneasy reality of allowing someone to know your fears, your flaws, and your dreams, all while understanding they have the choice to stay or walk away. It's terrifying. Vulnerability is always a risk. But it's also the foundation of the most meaningful connections. True friendship isn't built on perfection; it's built on courage—the courage to show up authentically and the willingness to let someone see the real you.

A FRIENDSHIP LIKE NO OTHER

Friendship with Jesus isn't surface-level; it's deeply intimate, honest, and transformative. Unlike human friendships that can waver, His friendship is steadfast, unchanging, and sacrificial. He doesn't just want obedience; He desires our hearts, our honesty, and our trust.

Throughout His ministry, Jesus didn't treat the disciples merely as students or followers—they were His friends. He understood them, empathized with their struggles, and walked alongside them. Even when their questions went unanswered, the intimacy of their relationship remained. An intimate friendship with Jesus teaches us to lean into trust, especially when clarity is absent. It's not about having every answer but about holding on to Him in every uncertainty.

When we approach Jesus, we must come as we are—honest, raw, and authentic. It's not about presenting perfection but building a relationship where we allow Him to see us fully. *Let El Roi be.* Speak your doubts aloud. Name your fears aloud. Grace meets us in the spaces where we're most imperfect. Bring your raw emotions—your anger, your confusion, your pain—directly to Him.

When clarity feels out of reach, keep showing up. Keep asking. Keep listening. Obedience matters, but Jesus desires connection, vulnerability, and shared relationship even more. You don't need flawless faith—just a faithful presence. Now, you may not always get it right, *I rarely get it right,* but He still wants to show up as your Friend. The closer we allow ourselves to be to Him, the more His character reshapes our hearts and our perspectives. Jesus doesn't just want to be your Savior; He wants to be your Friend. A Friend who listens, a Friend who understands, and a Friend who stays—no matter what. Will you let him?

REFLECTION QUESTIONS:

- How do you view your relationship with Jesus—as a servant, an acquaintance, or a friend?
- In what areas of your life do you need to invite Yeshua into deeper friendship?
- Are you willing to share your honest thoughts and emotions with Him?

"No longer do I call you slaves, for the slave does not know what his master is doing; but I have called you friends, because all things that I have heard from My Father I have made known to you."
John 15:15 (NASB)

Helper

Helper a distinctive title for the Holy Spirit in the Gospel of John (14:16, 26; 15:26; 16:7). The Helper, who could not come until Jesus departed (John 16:7), functions as the abiding presence of Jesus among His disciples (John 14:16–18). — *Holman Illustrated Bible Dictionary*

I MET A MAN.

We became friends.

It wasn't forced; it felt natural—like we'd known each other forever.

He understood me in ways I didn't think anyone could.

We got close—really close—until he had to leave.

He said it was something he had to handle for his Father.

Letting him go wasn't easy.

He wasn't just a friend; he became a teacher, a mentor—someone who carried wisdom I didn't even know I needed.

Watching him walk away felt heavier than I expected.

I knew where he was going, and deep down, I knew it would cost me something, too.

I watched his coat shift—white turning into this faded, almost bruised pink.

My chest felt tight. My heart broke.

But before he left, he said something that stuck with me.

He told me about You.

He said You'd be coming—someone who'd help me, guide me, walk with me.

He said I could trust You.

I trust him, I really do... but making new friends isn't easy for me.

I'm not great at opening up right away.

So, tell me—what are the rules here?

How does this partnership work?
Do I talk first, or do You?
Do I wait, or do I move?

Honestly, I'm not sure how to do this.
But I'm here... willing to try.

It's not easy for me.

I've been placed in this role of independence—a role I never asked for, never wanted.

Everyone thinks I'm strong enough to handle it all, that I'm capable of carrying this weight alone.

They call me wise, mature, the one who always seems to know what to do.

But you and I both know that's not true.

How do I tell them I'm tired?

How do I explain that I'm exhausted without sounding like I'm failing them?

Why can't they see it in my eyes—the way I'm begging for rest without saying a word?

How do they miss it every time?

Being the "toughest soldier" feels less like an honor and more like a sentence

I'll be honest—I want to isolate.

I know you might not be calling me to that,
but can I just have this one thing my way?
Can I disappear for a while?
Can I have a hall pass from being "the strong one"?

Please? Just for a little while.

All they do is take.
    They never pour into me.
    They never listen to me.
    They just see me as this strong friend,
    this strong child,
    this strong parent,
    this strong sibling.

I am not strong by choice.
    I am strong by experience.

Actually, I am not strong at all.
    My pillow knows best how strong I am not.
    My walls know by sound the weakness I feel.
    What do I do?

Why do I have to ask for what I freely give?
    Why do I have to request reciprocity?
    Why do I need to tell them I am hurting?

It's not fair.
    I endure and still pray for them.
    I endure and still war for them.
    I endure and still show up for them.

Do they think I am not in need?

Okay... I'll admit it.
    You're right.

I crave connection. I crave relationship.
    I don't want to be alone—not really.

But saying it out loud feels impossible.
    Those four letters—L.O.V.E—get stuck in my throat,
    and my hands freeze before they can type them out.
    Because wanting it? Needing it? That's easy.

But asking for it and not receiving it?
    That's a different kind of pain.
    That's a rejection I'm not sure I can handle.

I am confused.
    I am not happy though everything is well.
    I feel a void.
    It's growing deeper and wider than I can contain.
    I seek darkness.
    I seek the shadows.

I cannot tell anyone the depths of this darkness
    because they do not understand.
    They see things going well and I have no reason to complain
    but in spite of this, I feel empty.
    I feel something missing.

I am here but are You?
    I am here but where exactly is here?

They look to me for answers, but honestly... I don't have them.

They're trying to figure out how I'm still standing,
 but the truth is—I fight myself every single day.

I don't know why I feel this way.
 I don't know why I'm unhappy.
 I don't know why I keep craving isolation.

I need help.

This heaviness keeps coming back.
 I don't want it anymore.
 I feel it—the weight sinking in my stomach,
 the tightness crawling up my throat,
 like I might break apart if I let it out.

What is this?
 Where is this coming from?
 Please... help me.

I've done what You asked of me.
 I've given what I thought was required.

But is there more?
 Is there still something clinging to me that doesn't belong?

· · ·

Is it me?

I try to tell them—I'm not well.

But they just tilt their heads, offer a nervous laugh, or brush it off like I'm being dramatic.

They don't understand.

They don't understand the weight I carry when I step into that space.

They don't understand how heavy it feels just to exist around them sometimes.

It's not just tiredness—it's draining.

It's not just discomfort—it's suffocating.

They see me smiling.

They see the space tidy, the tasks done, the surface-level signs of someone who's "holding it together."

But spiritually? Spiritually, I'm crumbling.

I'm not okay.

The atmosphere feels thick, like something pressing down on my chest.

I can't breathe deeply there.

I can't find peace there.

It's as if something invisible is pulling me down, and no one else seems to notice.

They don't see the internal battle I fight every time I step into that place.

They don't see how I have to force myself to stay, to smile, to speak when all I want is to run.

Spiritually, I'm not just tired—I'm empty.

And emptiness feels loud in a place where everyone assumes you're fine.

But how do I explain that?

How do I tell them that while everything looks fine on the outside, something inside of me feels like it's slowly withering away?

How do I tell them without sounding ungrateful, dramatic, or "too much"?

I'm not okay.

And I wish they could see it without me having to spell it out.

I've been coming to this café every day since He left.

There's an older man who comes here daily too.

Same time, same corner seat.

I watch him order a sandwich and a cup of coffee, like clockwork.

He always smirks, just a little—like he knows a secret the rest of us missed.

He looks... content.

He looks... at peace.

But is it real peace?

What is real peace, anyway?

I've smiled before—right after wiping away tears in a bathroom mirror.

I've prayed for others while silently wondering if my own prayers were just bouncing off the ceiling.

Is his peace steady, or does it tremble underneath like mine does?

Is it a calm he's earned, or one he's pretending to wear?

Should I speak to him?

Should I check in on him?

Or maybe... maybe he's already noticed me too.

You know, You don't respond to me like Them.

I'm sitting here waiting—
 like I'm next to an old house phone,
 hoping my crush might finally call.

When My Friend spoke of You,
 He described You as warm, steady, and safe.
 He said You were the missing piece—
 the part of me that would feel whole when You arrived.

But right now...
 I feel like I'm sitting alone in an open field,
 beneath the shade of a tree,
 whispering words into the wind,
 hoping it'll carry them to You.

I watch the sky for some kind of sign.
 A shift in the clouds.
 A distant rumble.
 A breeze that feels different.

But nothing happens.
 No signal.
 No sound.
 Just silence.

Are You listening?
 Are You here?

Why is destiny so heavy?
 What's so urgent about what is destined to be?
 Why so serious?
 Why is everything a
 choice between life and death?
 Every decision requires counsel,
 yet every decision is still mine to make.

Destiny doesn't come with a map?

Cafe Man is back.

But today, he didn't order anything.
    He just sat down with a book,
    quiet and steady, like he belonged there.

Before he left, though,
    he did something I didn't expect.

He paid the bill for a woman and her kids.
    No big speech.
    No attention drawn to himself.
    Just a simple gesture—paid in full.

It all happened so fast,
    the woman didn't even get the chance to thank him.
    But he didn't seem to mind.
    Recognition didn't seem to be the point.

I wonder if he knew I was watching.

To be "light" is more than flipping a switch.
   To be "light" means being consistent or better yet committed.
   To give up you for the sake of them.

No one ever asks Light
   if it needs a break,
   if it needs a chance to regain strength.

No one cares about Light until
   it's missing.
   The absence of what is makes them question,
   and even miss what was.

If My Friend left You here with me,
  why don't You speak to me?
  He may have spoken in riddles,
  but He spoke.
  You seem mute.
  Are You just here as a shadow?
  Are You just a watcher?
  Are You waiting for something to
  happen to make your grand entrance?

When will You really help me?

How do I know if it's You or me talking?
    How do I decipher my conscious from your lead?
    The voice sounds the same.

It's getting hard to breathe here.
  I don't like people.
  I mean, I do but, it's draining.

You told me to be in community,
  but community feels like an emotional battlefield.
  So many feelings, so many unspoken things.
  It's heavy.

I notice the elephants in the room,
  the flies on the wall,
  the things no one says out loud.

So, I keep my distance.
  I avoid deep conversations.
  I avoid building connections.

Because eventually, I'll see too much.
  I'll know too much.

And honestly, carrying that kind of insight—it's exhausting.

Okay, it's not just the weight of their emotions
    that pushes me away.

But hear me out, they hurt me.

They violate my body.
    They violate my space.
    And I'm still expected to have faith.
    So can I?
    Speak faith while enduring trauma that volume could not force to stop.

How did You share the truth in the midst of the ridicule?
    How? How did You still love Your father that gave You an impossible task for people who would never appreciate it?

I need Your help in this.
    It's bigger than me.
    It feels too great for me to carry and I have no choice in the matter.
    I can't walk away because I'm tied to him like You are. When I'm away from Him, my heart aches.
    My ears are stuffed.
    I become anxious. Darkness sets in. So I have to press. I have to endure the pruning if I want to be near Him.

I am growing tired of that word—endure.
    When do I get to bask? When do I get to rest?

Did You ever want to stop?
   Did You ever feel the same?
   Did You wish for a moment of imperfection,
   a chance to just be human?

Was it hard, being perfect?
   Being the only one, the blueprint,
   and still, everyone thinks You're the counterfeit?

I'm trying. No, I'm really trying.
   It feels like everything is coming together just to make me fail.
   Like it's all closing in.

I'm carrying blame for things I haven't even done,
   and it's not fair. It's unjust.
   While they walk away unscathed.

You said it.
    It wasn't me.
    You put that idea
    in my heart.
    You planted that
    thought.
    I was fine before
    You gave me hope
    It was possible.
    You gave me hope
    I could do it.
    You gave me hope
    to seek.

So why if
    You knew I'd receive
    rejection?
    Why give me hope
    then leave me feeling
    unworthy
    unqualified
    less than.

I inherited your imagination.
    Why plant the seed
    for it to not grow?
    Why plant the seed
    where only
    pain seems
    to be watering
    it?

Do You hear me?
    Do You see me?
    Do You feel me?

You give me dreams—
    dreams that torment my reality,
    dreams just out of my reach.

You've planted them
    deep within my heart.

But my heart,
    it's been tainted.
    I've trusted before,
    but it only led me down painful paths.

I can't carry
    more false hope.

I DID MORE than say it. I see it.
You look in front of you and what are you seeing?
No really, what do you see?
What are you feeling?
Notice the tension in your shoulders.
Notice the clench of your jaw.
Notice the overwhelming need to scream.

Now, think of me. Think of that dream.
Close your eyes and follow me.
Now tell me what you see.
Notice what you feel.
Notice your breathing has slowed.
Notice your hand holding mine.

Keep your eyes closed and walk with Me.
Keep your eyes closed and talk with Me.

Yesterday, the storm came strong,
  leaves and branches swept along.
  The wind, it roared with wild intent,
  while I stood still, a quiet event.

The waves, they crashed upon the shore,
  while others ran, I stayed once more.
  A beauty found in nature's song,
  as elements in harmony belonged.

The heatwave broke, a chill took place,
  seagulls gathered in tranquil grace.
  When rain did slow, I felt His near,
  a covenant like a halo clear.

My heart was filled with grateful cries,
  for in that moment, I realized—
  He truly hears, He knows my plea,
  His presence still surrounds me, free.

That night, it wasn't like Daniel.
    I felt the fire, and it burned me—
    leaving scars only I can see.

You left me vulnerable.
    I begged, three times I begged,
    but when You finally came,
    it was too late.
    A part of me was taken—
    my words, forced from my lips,
    prayers became whispers
    until they faded into silence.

If You knew how that night would unfold,
    why didn't You speak up?
    If You knew what would happen to me,
    why didn't You protect me?
    Why let that predator into my space?

The next morning, it all hit me.
    Embarrassment.
    Betrayal.
    I replayed every moment,
    thinking I did everything right.
    But the voice, that soulless voice,
    still echoes in my mind.
    I can still see them.

That room became a museum,
    and my face—the exhibit,
    displaying the horrors of that night.

It turned into a rerun I never asked for,
an endless loop of pain.
My enemy turned my friends against me.
They abandoned me.
They talked about what happened.
And left me to relive it.

So where were You, my help?
    Why did You leave me alone?
    In the darkness, I found comfort—
    but it was the kind that eats away at you.
    Guilt followed me.
    Shame wrapped itself around me.
    And brokenness poured out of me.

Fall upon me,
  walk with me,
  guide me,
  be my strength and help me break free from sin.

Where I have compromised my faith and walked away from Christ,
  convict me, correct me, and restore me.
  Abide in me, that I may burn with a desire to do Your will.
  God, I repent for only accepting Christ as Savior,
  but not fully embracing Him as Lord.
  For rejecting the Holy Spirit, my guide and help,
  I turn to You today, seeking refuge in Your arms.

Abide in me, as I abide in You.
  I no longer want my will,
  but let Your will be done in my life.
  Change my words to reflect Yours,
  change my ways to align with Yours.

In Jesus Name, Amen.

YOU ARE worth so much more than you realize.
   There is more of Me in you than you know.
   There was nothing wrong with you—
   what was wrong was the way the world tried to shape you.
   I couldn't stop you from going through it,
   because you wouldn't have been ready to return home without
experiencing it first.

I need you to understand,
   My Help doesn't always feel like an immediate rescue.
   Sometimes, My Help comes in the form of growth.
   It comes through development,
   through building something lasting.
   It's about the journey,
   not just the quick fix.
   And I'm here for all of it,
   with you.

I LONG to hear Your voice,
    Your still, quiet voice.
    What I hear now is not You—
    it's confusion, it's chaos.

I'd rather You speak in parables,
    like You did with Your disciples—
    then I'd know it's truly You.
    Why are these voices so loud?

Why do they torment me so?
    They won't stop,
    I can't make them be quiet.

Please, whatever isn't from You,
    take it away from me now.

I repent for doing it. I repent for knowing what was right and not doing what was right.

I don't want to do it. I really don't.
	Help me to fight to live.
	Please,

just

	help me

					to fight

									to live.

I can't do it myself.
	The pain in my chest won't calm with my coaching anymore.
	The tears won't obey me.
	My breathing isn't controlled by me anymore.

Hide me, I want to be away from everyone and every care. Help me, please.

I know I won't make it, if I give in right now.
	I am trying to bear my cross, but it's trying to kill me.

Please?

What are You trying to draw out of me?
    What is so precious within me,
    that this brutal journey has become my path?

Let me partner with You in getting in.
    Maybe I can help find it for You.
    Maybe I can show You it's not as deep as it seems.
    Help me understand what it is that You see in me.

I feel like I'm being cut, burned, and broken.
    When does the healing begin?
    When does my peace arrive?
    When does my happiness come?

When will my comfort find its way to me?

Do I get my happy ending?
    I prayed them through their deliverance
    and healing like You told me.
    Am I only helping everyone find theirs?
    I stood in the gap.
    I interceded, but what about me?
    Who is interceding for me?
    Who is warring for me?

I want peace.
    Will I ever experience peace?
    I know the promise You set for Your people, but
    is the promise for me too?

Is it?

Yesterday, I was set out.
    No home, no place to rest.
    They mock me, they laugh—
    because somehow, I still have the audacity
    to pray in Your name.

You said if I called, You'd help me.
    But it feels like all I ever get
    is the answering machine—
    ironically, of course.

I can't help but to cry now.

Years of holding it all in and smiling is up to me.

Nowhere feels safe anymore.

I've become a safe place for everyone else and my own body leaves me uncertain.

Is happiness even for me?

I've attached it to everyone else

for so long that I don't know

how to measure it on my own.

I don't know why its so unattainable.

I want to choose me but family and religion has me in a chokehold.

I don't want to leave God.

I want him without man's involvement.

This world feels so constraining.

I feel like my own thoughts and feelings are sinful.

I've messed up so much that crying over it seems ungodly.

I am tired of trying to make everyone else proud and accept me.

I feel like a disappointment.

I want to get things right so bad

and I just can't.

Why do I allow people to hurt me? Why do people hurt me?

Breaking in plain sight and fighting to breathe but it is hard. I am losing.

Time heals all wounds, right?

But I don't even think that's scripture.

I am scared to share the truth.

scared this will be my only chance.
scared the truth will cause hurt at the expense of

healing me.

Is that fair?

Two hours on the phone—
    I didn't realize how much I needed it.
    You spoke through a friend,
    one who doesn't even believe in You.

My introverted nature almost
    let the call go unanswered,
    but You nudged me to pick up.
    You really do use willing vessels,
    no matter how far
    they seem from You.

How much longer before You help me?
    I've changed.
    I've fled.
    I've repented.
    So why am I still not given Your peace?

Why do I keep reliving what I want to heal from?
    Why does it feel like You're ignoring this pain?
    I've prayed for those who hurt me—because You asked me to.
    I've prayed for their families too.
    But why does it feel like no one is praying for me?
    No one seems to understand.
    Forgiving someone who never cared about the damage they caused—
    it's heavy.
    Two years, and I still carry what I never wanted.
    I still see their face.
    I called out for help then, just like I'm calling now.
    Help came late before...
    Will it ever come again?

I haven't slept through the night in three days,
  unable to quiet my thoughts enough to find the lullaby to peace.
  They've spoken Your Word to me, but why does it feel so distant from this experience?
  Why does redemption feel so unreachable?
  Why is recovery from what was done so hard?
  I've denied my desires for days, and yet all I'm left with is more guilt and shame.
  You say, "Believe" and "Have faith."
  And I did.
  I believed You could and would.
  I had faith in Your rescue.
  But look at me—I'm still here.
  I'm suffering.
  How much longer do I "believe" and "have faith" before I call it quits?

Tell me, how do I endure this new space of surrender?
  How do I carry the weight of a past that taunts me every time I call on Your name?

Do You love me?
  How can You love me and not rescue me from this pain?
  How can You love me and watch this torment unfold?

Please, answer me.
  Don't stay silent.
  I need to know You hear me.
  I need to know You see me.
  Please... see me.
  Please.

Okay, maybe I did need to just pray.
    Prayer always pulls me back to You.

It feels like You've been sitting at this table,
    waiting—arms crossed, not in frustration,
    but in patience.
    Like You knew I'd show up eventually,
    even if I was late.

You didn't leave.
    You didn't roll Your eyes or sigh in disappointment.
    You stayed.
    You stayed because You knew—
    somehow, someway—I'd walk in,
    messy, tired, and carrying too much weight.

When I finally sat down,
    You didn't lecture me.
    You didn't point at the clock.
    You just opened Your arms,
    and I fell into them.

And I cried.

I cried because You waited.
    I cried because You didn't have to.
    I cried because You still choose me,
    still trust me,
    still believe in me.

. . .

But I'm scared.

I know You're calling me to step forward,
    to stand on the frontlines with You leading the way.
    But I'm scared.
    My knees shake just thinking about it.

So, I prayed.

I prayed You'd hold on tight,
    that You'd never let go of my hand,
    even if I start slipping,
    even if I hesitate,
    even if I'm late again.

I wonder if He shows us dreams
    in pieces we can handle—
    if He speaks in fragments
    so we don't shatter under the weight of the whole picture.

Is He stretching me past my limits,
    or just showing me the limits I've built around myself?

Lately, I've been dreaming more.
    I know He's speaking,
    but every time, I second-guess it.

I read about a boy who dreamed once.
    His vision made no sense to the people closest to him.
    They heard and dismissed him.
    They heard and turned on him.
    They heard and sold him away.

An unusual dream—
    and it cost him everything.

Was it sharing the dream
    that set his story in motion?
    Or was it simply having the dream at all?

Did the dream carry a price,
    or was it the faith to believe in it that came with a cost?

It feels a little unhinged,
    a bit like madness—
    to expect someone
    who doesn't know You,
    who doesn't recognize Your voice,
    to live by Your words,
    to hold to Your standards.

It's like building a house on sand
    and wondering why it crumbles.

Your Word says,
    Faith comes by hearing,
    and hearing by the Word of God.
    But how can he have faith
    when he doesn't recognize the Word—
    not in flesh,
    not in spirit,
    not in truth?

He sees the Father,
    but not the Son—
    the Savior who came,
    who stayed,
    who saved.

God, it's driving me mad.
    I see it now.
    I get it.

.   .   .

Unequally yoked isn't just advice—
    it's a warning.
    There's no middle ground,
    no both/and.
    It's either or.

No compromise.
    No blending light with shadow.
    It's clear.

And yet...
    it still hurts.

I'm angry. Deep, simmering, righteous anger.
    Am I wrong for this?
    Is this my flesh speaking, or is it You—
    prompting me, stirring me, pushing me forward?

Confirm my next step.
    I refuse to move until You speak.
    I won't take another step into this fog
    without Your word lighting the way.

I'm sick of this feeling.
    Sick of the silence.
    Sick of straining to hear You
    while everyone else seems to have Your voice on speed dial.
    Why does everyone hear You about me... except me?
    That doesn't feel right.
    That doesn't sound like You.

The truth is—I'm not happy.
    I haven't been.
    I've been surviving, yes.
    Content, maybe.
    But joy? Peace? Fulfillment?
    No.

And the agreement we made in the summer of 2022?
    It feels... broken.
    Like a thread snapped under too much tension.
    And now I'm left holding the loose ends,
    wondering if I misunderstood,
    or if You changed Your mind.

.   .   .

Did You ever feel this way?
    Did You ever look at the weight You carried
    and wonder if the promise at the end
    was worth the breaking in the middle?

Speak to me.
    Please.

THE CAFE MAN spoke to me today. I hadn't expected it—our conversations are usually brief, casual, about the weather or his usual sandwich. But today, he paused, and his words took me by surprise.

"The sticker on your laptop always brings me hope." He happens to be just as observant as I am.

I looked at the sticker for a moment. "Jesus Loves You." It's simple, yet in its simplicity, it seems to carry weight, especially for someone like him. He continued, his voice quiet, almost distant as he shared his story.

"I don't always feel like He does," his eyes downcast. "I've made decisions that cost me my family. Decisions I know were His will. My family rejected me for it. My wife wanted nothing to do with my new belief. But, I had an encounter with Him that I could not deny. I could not shake."

He paused, as if weighing his words carefully. "Being the head of your family, looked at as the leader, is a heavy burden when you're not well enough to lead. But men aren't always given the space to communicate that truth. And even if we are, we're often viewed as weak or inadequate. I wrestled with those thoughts for years. I did everything I was supposed to do—I provided for my family, loved my wife, and never broke my vows. I checked every box as a husband, as a father. I gave my all, but they never saw it. And when they didn't respect me, I endured. Because a man is supposed to be able to take it."

His voice faltered for a moment, and I could see the strain in his eyes. I could feel the rawness in his confession.

"After years of enduring, you get tired of just taking it. You get tired of carrying the weight with no relief. Men are expected to keep going, no matter how broken we feel inside, and we're not given the space to release without fearing we'll be seen as less than. It's exhausting."

His eyes met mine, and for a moment, there was a deep sadness, a longing in them. I could sense his pain, but also a glimmer of something else—hope.

"One day, after I'd left work, I was broken. This hole I'd been masking for so long began to expand, and I knew that if I didn't do something, it would engulf me. I took a risk. I prayed. I didn't know what I was doing, but I called out, 'Whoever is out there, I need help. I can't do this on my own. Will You help me?'"

He swallowed, and I could hear the vulnerability in his voice.

"I didn't expect much. But then, my father called. A man who's never been expressive—never once said he loved me in thirty-three years—he called and poured his heart out. He told me he loved me, and apologized for shutting me out. I couldn't believe it. I couldn't believe that someone so close to me felt the same way I did. That I wasn't alone."

He took a deep breath, letting the weight of the moment settle.

"After we talked, I felt a relief, but the heaviness was still there. On my way home, I passed a group of teenagers with signs that said, 'If you need help, we have help.' It seemed like a sign. I pulled over, and those kids—those kids—prayed for me. They prayed for my healing, my restoration. How did they know? How could they possibly know what I was going through?"

His voice trembled again, his eyes glistening with emotion.

"One of the young men said, 'He sees you. You are a great father and leader, but He doesn't want you to endure it on your own.' And that's when I broke down. I cried like a child in the arms of their father."

I could hear the sincerity in his voice, the awe in his words.

"I knew then that I couldn't deny Him. I wanted to know more about this God who saw me, who cared for me. But it cost me. It cost me my family. I thought I could go back, but the truth I found wouldn't let me. It's hard. It's painful. But today, I started to grieve the loss of them. And then, I saw your laptop."

He smiled faintly, gesturing toward the sticker again.

"Thank you," he said softly.

I didn't know how to respond. His words had shaken me, and in that moment, I understood something deeper about faith, about the sacrifices we make, and about the hope that can come in the most unexpected places.

The sticker, so simple yet powerful, had carried more weight than I could have imagined.

And maybe, just maybe, it was never just a sticker. It was a reminder. A message. That sometimes, the hardest parts of our journey are the ones that bring us closest to Him.

Jesus loves you.

It's a simple truth that, in the end, changes everything.

My Reflection

TALKING to the Holy Spirit and allowing Him to lead and guide can be more challenging than it seems. If you're anything like me, you may struggle with distinguishing whether it's really the Holy Spirit speaking or just your intuition. Or maybe, they can be one and the same? Over the years, as I've longed to hear His voice clearly, there were moments when I couldn't discern the tone of His voice. I didn't yet understand the language of His voice. It wasn't until I invested time in building a relationship with Him that I began to distinguish His voice from my own desires.

It's similar to dating. The more time you spend with someone, the better you understand their communication style, even in the smallest things. For example, a simple "sure" can mean more than just agreement. It can feel passive, like something's off, and often, there's something wrong beneath the surface. But you'd never know that unless you've spent time truly understanding them. The same is true with the Holy Spirit—spending time in relationship with Him is the key to hearing and recognizing His voice.

EMBRACING THE HELPER: FINDING GUIDANCE IN OUR STRUGGLES

As I sit to reflect on my journey, I can't help but share with you the lessons I've learned, the lessons that have shaped my understanding of the Helper and how He moves in our lives. The moments I've shared are not just one of struggle or triumph, but a glimpse into the way the Helper works—quietly, patiently, and often in ways we least expect.

Take the story of the Cafe Man, for instance. Although he was a fictional encounter, (and yes, I decided to use a fictional encounter similar to parables like Jesus used to teach a lesson) he arrived in my life on a day I wasn't expecting any kind of change. But as we spoke, something shifted within me. I began to understand a deeper truth about the Helper: He doesn't only show up in dramatic moments of deliverance. He shows up in the quiet spaces, in the waiting, and in the ordinary moments—often in places where we think He isn't working at all. Through the Cafe Man, I saw that the Helper is always at work, even in the most unexpected encounters, shaping us in ways we may not fully recognize until later.

1. Patience and Presence

One of the first things, we can learn from the Cafe Man is the power of patience. Cafe Man shares how, despite everything he had been through, God had never rushed him. And I realized then that God is never in a hurry. He waits for us—sometimes for years. He waits with open arms, not in frustration, but in anticipation. The Helper doesn't rush us through our pain or healing; He stays present, patiently waiting for us to come back to Him.

2. Vulnerability as Strength

The Cafe Man wasn't afraid to admit that he was broken. He

spoke about the pressure he felt to be the strong one for his family, the one who had it all together. But when he allowed himself to be vulnerable, he found strength—not in his own power, but in God's. This reveals a truth we sometimes haven't seen before: vulnerability is not a sign of weakness, but a key to healing. The Helper meets us in our brokenness and shows us that it's okay to be weak in order to experience His strength.

When we open up, we give the Helper space to work. And He is working—whether we realize it or not.

3. The Power of Listening

One of the most profound lessons I've learned is that the Helper listens—deeply. The way the Cafe Man's story unfolded made me realize that God is always listening, even when I think no one is. The prayer that the young people prayed for him, the encouragement they spoke over him—that was God listening and speaking through them. I've come to see that the Helper often works through others to reach us, and we need to be open to hearing from those who might not look like the answer we expect.

I've learned to be a better listener, not just to God but to those around me. I've learned to recognize that the Helper can speak through anyone, in any moment.

4. Unexpected Sources of Help

The Cafe Man's encounter with those teenagers on the street was one of the most unexpected sources of help I've ever heard of. I think about this often because it reminds me that God's help comes in ways I don't always anticipate. The way help showed up for him wasn't in a church or through a counselor, but through a group of kids who didn't even know his story. Yet, they prayed for him, and their prayers were exactly what he needed.

Help isn't always packaged the way we think it should be. We may look for answers in certain places, but the Helper can use anyone, anything, at any time to bring us the peace we need. Are you open to it?

5. Healing Through Community

Healing often comes through community. It's through the unexpected support of sometimes strangers that begins our healing. The Helper uses community, not just for support but for our restoration. We don't have to do this alone. Even in our isolation, God is moving through those around us, bringing healing through relationships.

6. Sacrifice and Cost

There is a cost of following the truth. Deciding to be Spirit-led and obedient will always come at a cost. For Cafe Man, it meant losing his family, but in return, he found something far greater. The Holy Spirit doesn't promise an easy life—He promises that we will never be alone in our sacrifices, He will help. And sometimes, the hardest part of our journey is choosing the truth, knowing it may lead to loss.

7. Hope in Darkness

The Cafe Man's experience reminds us that the Helper never leaves us in darkness. Even when he felt completely lost, even when he felt rejected, God's presence was there, bringing hope. The young man's words to him—"He sees you"—reminded him that God was with him, even in the darkest times. El Roi, the Hebrew name for God, meaning the God who sees.

God sees me, sees you, sees all of us. And He is working, even when we can't see it.

My prayer for you, as you read these words, is that you would recognize the Helper in your own life. That you would see the quiet ways He is moving, and that you would allow Him to be the source of your strength, your peace, and your healing.

Trust me, He is always there—waiting with open arms for you to come home.

Reflection Questions:

- How have you experienced God's patience in your life, especially during times of silence or waiting? How can this inspire you to be patient with yourself and others?
- Reflect on a time when you felt the weight of trying to be strong for others. How did it affect you, and what would it look like to allow yourself to be vulnerable in that situation?
- How has community played a role in your healing process? Are there ways you can open yourself to others' support, or offer your own support to someone in need?
- Have you ever felt lost or overwhelmed? What gave you hope during that time, and how can you hold on to that hope in future struggles?

every stage
isn't pretty
some left
more scars
than others
some left
holes man could
never fill

every stage
came with loss
and tears
laughter and lies
pain and regret
prayers and conviction

every stage
came with
a
breaking

every stage
played it's part
in getting
me to where
God needed
me to
be

His Beloved

Then Peter, turning around,
saw the disciple whom Jesus loved following,
who also had leaned on His breast at the supper...
John 21:20

Epilogue

DEAR READER,

What if I told you, God already knew it would happen? He knew you'd experience that pain and hurt. He knew you'd give your heart to a person and they wouldn't value it? What if I told you, He knew they would lie on you? He knew they would slander your name and defile your character. What if I told you, He wanted it all to happen?

That he placed a ram on that cross, so you wouldn't be placed there. What if I told you, God came here in flesh (Jesus), to live a sinless life for you to be able to find true hope, healing, and eternal life.

These words in this book aren't fictional. They are conversations I've had with God the Father, God the Son, and God the Holy Spirit. In different moments of my life, I found speaking to one was more comforting than speaking to the other. Do not mistake this as me saying they are separate. No, they are all one, but who I address provided a different form of intimacy in my prayers.

As you read these conversations, I pray you find a way to start your own conversation with God. I pray you start an honest conversation with Him. If God is all-knowing, there is nothing you need to conceal when coming to him. If God is love and He loves unconditionally, there is nothing you can say that will cause him to stop loving you. Yes, we can sin, and sin can place us further from God, but if we repent, by God's grace only we can be made new. Our sins hurt God just as much as it hurts us, but unlike our friends, family, or partners, God will not hold it against us.

My ask: when you read, allow yourself to be vulnerable with God.

Jade Juana Polly

The Word of God tells us to "meditate on His word day and night." (Psalms 1:2) To meditate, biblically, is a combination between studying scripture and praying scripture. We must speak the Word of God to ourselves to become familiar with it. When we know the Word of God we know how to respond to our circumstances by the Word of God.

Acceptance & Purpose
John 17:9-14
Romans 8:1
1 Corinthians 1:30
Ephesians 1:3-6
Jeremiah 29:11
Isaiah 43:1
Proverbs 29:21
Ephesians 2:10
1 Peter 2:9
2 Timothy 1:9
Colossians 1:16

Anxiety
Psalm 55:22
Isaiah 26:3
Psalm 94:19
Proverbs 12:25
Philipians 4:6-7
Matthew 6:34
1 Peter 5:7
John 14:1
Luke 12:25-26

Comfort & Grief
Psalm 10:17
Psalm 94:19
Isaiah 61:1

Confusion
Proverbs 3:5-6
Isaiah 26:3
Isaiah 55:8-9
1 Corinthians 14:33
James 1:5
John 16:13

Depression & Suicide
Psalm 30:5
Psalm 55:22
Lamentations 3:22-24
John 16:33
Revelation 21:4
Psalm 139:13-14
Romans 8:38-39

Fear
Isaiah 41:10
Psalm 34:4
Deuteronomy 31:6
2 Timothy 1:7
Matthew 6:34
John 14:27
Matthew 10:28
Luke 12:32
Romans 8:15
Hebrews 13:6

Forgiveness
Psalm 103:10-12
Isaiah 1:18
Micah 7:18-19
Daniel 9:9
Matthew 6:14-15
Ephesians 4:32
Luke 17:3-4
Mark 11:25
Luke 22:34

Love
Deuteronomy 6:5
Leviticus 19:18
Psalm 136:1
Proverbs 10:12
Matthew 22:37-39

Peace
Isaiah 26:3
Psalm 29:11
Numbers 6:24-26
John. 14:27
Romans 5:1
Ephesians 2:14
Colossians 3:15
Matthew 5:9
Romans 15:13
James 3:18
2 Thessalonians 3:16
John 15:13
Romans 5:8
1 John 4:7-8
1 John 4:19
Ephesians 3:17-19

Forgiveness
Psalm 103:10-12
Isaiah 1:18
Micah 7:18-19
Daniel 9:9
Matthew 6:14-15
Ephesians 4:32
Luke 17:3-4
Mark 11:25
Luke 22:34

Love
Deuteronomy 6:5
Leviticus 19:18
Psalm 136:1
Proverbs 10:12
Matthew 22:37-39
John 15:13
Romans 5:8
1 John 4:7-8
1 John 4:19
Ephesians 3:17-19

Truth & Wisdom
John 14:6
John 17:17
Colossians 1:5-6, 23
2 Timothy 2:19
Proverbs 2:6-22
Proverbs 9:10
Colossians 2:2-3
James 1:5
Colossians 2:2-3
1 Corinthians 1:30

www.ingramcontent.com/pod-product-compliance
Lightning Source LLC
Chambersburg PA
CBHW070534090426
42735CB00013B/2980